D1516571

# A POCKETFUL
# OF LUXURY
# ITALIAN HOTELS

# A POCKETFUL OF LUXURY ITALIAN HOTELS

Photography and Text by Panagiotis Fotiadis

images
Publishing

Published in Australia in 2007 by
The Images Publishing Group Pty Ltd
ABN 89 059 734 431
6 Bastow Place, Mulgrave, Victoria 3170,
Australia
Tel: +61 3 9561 5544  Fax: +61 3 9561 4860
books@imagespublishing.com
www.imagespublishing.com

National Library of Australia Cataloguing-in-
Publication entry:

Fotiadis, Panagiotis.
Pocketful of luxury Italian hotels.

ISBN 978 1 86470 2699 (hbk.).

1. Hotels - Italy. 2. Luxury. I. Title. (Series :
Pocketful series (Images Publishing Group)).

728.50945

Edited by Melina Deliyannis

Designed by The Graphic Image Studio Pty Ltd,
Mulgrave, Australia
www.tgis.com.au

Digital production by Splitting Image Studio
Pty Ltd, Melbourne
Printed by Everbest Printing Co Ltd. In Hong
Kong/China

IMAGES has included on its website a page for
special notices in relation to this and its other
publications. Please visit
www.imagespublishing.com

# Contents

# Contents continued

Projects

# Hotel Palazzo Sasso
## Ravello

*Via San Giovanni
del Toro 28
84010 Ravello*

*Tel + 39 089 81 81 81
Fax + 39 089 85 89 00*

*www.palazzosasso.com*

While it can't be touched nor can the swashing of the waves be heard, one falls in love with the vastness of the sea below the terrace of the Hotel Palazzo Sasso, which is more than 400 metres away. High above the Amalfi Coast in the medieval mountain-top village of Ravello, one feels closer to the sky than to the earth. On the same sun-kissed terrace 120 years ago, Richard Wagner completed his last opera, *Parsifal,* and likened the place to the fabled magic garden of Klingsor. Half a century later, it was here that DH Lawrence worked on *Lady Chatterley's Lover*. In the 1950s many celebrities found their earthly paradise in this place. This 12th-century palazzo has been one of Europe's best hotels since the 1880s. Closed during the 1980s, the Hotel Palazzo Sasso was fully restored by the Virgin Group, and re-opened in July 1997 to continue its historic adventure.

# Il San Pietro di Positano
## Positano

Via Laurito 2
84017 Positano

Tel +39 089 875455
Fax +39 089 811449

www.ilsanpietro.it

Would one ever imagine that an enormous 90-metre-high rock could be transformed into a small hotel utopia? Carlo Cinque not only conceived it but made his dream come true. Il San Pietro di Positano has justifiably been recognised as an architectural triumph because it is positioned on a massive rough cliff. Its large terrace takes advantage of the magnificent views of the famous Positano, the isle of Li Galli and the town of Praiano. Every room is carefully tucked into the cliff face, offering endless views of the Amalfi Coast. The rooms are large and luxurious, each one individually decorated with cool, hand-painted tile floors and elegant pieces of art and antiques. On arrival, guests are enticed by the scents and colours of flowers. Their fascinating fragrance and beauty extend from the reception area down to the cliff edges and the private beach.

## Le Sirenuse
### Positano

*Via C. Colombo 30*
*84017 Positano*
*Tel +39 089 87 50 66*
*Fax +39 089 81 17 98*
*www.sirenuse.it*

Le Sirenuse is a hotel on the Amalfi Coast that lures its guests in much the same way as the Sirens of Greek mythology. Parthenhope, Leucosia and Ligeia lured sailors to their deaths with their enchanting song. They tempted curious Odysseus with their melodious voices, lyre and flute but he escaped by having his sailors plug their ears with beeswax and tie him to the mast. When Jason and the Argonauts passed by their island, Orpheus, the greatest musician of the ancient world, prevented the crew from being lured by drowning out the Sirens' voices when he played his music more beautifully than they. These winged ladies survive in the blue sea of archipelago Li Galli in the form of little islands. However, these days their sweet song comes from the charismatic Le Sirenuse. This distinguished, super-chic hotel in the heart of picturesque Positano has long held a special allure. 'It bites deep. It is a dream place that isn't quite real when you're there and becomes beckoningly real after you have gone', wrote John Steinbeck.

# Capri Palace Hotel & Spa
## Capri

Via Capodimonte 2b
80071 Anacapri

Tel +39 081 978 0111
Fax +39 081 837 3191

www.capripalace.com

Emperor Caesar Augustus used the name 'Apragopolis' for the island of Capri, which can be translated as 'the land of sweet idleness'. Eight centuries earlier, Anacapri, the Acropolis of the island, was created by a group of peaceful Greek settlers who carved a long, steep staircase into the rocky slope of Monte Solaro from the coastline. Nowadays, from this dominant position, which offers great panoramic views over the Bay of Naples and the island of Ischia, the Capri Palace Hotel & Spa is rapidly becoming the new elite address on Capri. A recent re-styling, inspired by the simple elegance of classical Mediterranean architecture, has been combined with tradition, history and cultivated ambience. White-coloured suites with shades of brown, blue and green are named Acropolis, Athena, Megaron, Andromeda, Callas, Monroe and Warhol.

# Continentale
## Florence

*Vicolo dell'Oro 6/R*
*Florence 50123*
*Tel +39 055 27262*
*Fax +39 055 283139*
*www.lungarnohotels.com*

Florence, New York, Madrid, Hong Kong … places and time coexist in a rather modest living room where a scattered collection of clocks and watches has been transformed into stylish coffee tables. Minutes and seconds simultaneously strike the time of all the big cities worldwide creating a unique time zone.

The Continentale, one of Florence's boutique hotels, is a modern interpretation of *La Dolce Vita's* Italy of the 1950s. The little cozy Lounge Bar is open to the public as well as hotel guests. Admirers of Renaissance art can relax and have a drink after their visit to the Uffizi Gallery before continuing on to the Palazzo Vecchio or the Duomo. Comfortably stretched out on a chaise longue in the Sala Relax, guests have the privilege of watching the lively passeggiata on the Ponte Vecchio and the surrounding streets, from an entirely exclusive position. The Sky Lounge, with an extraordinary view of the Arno River, the Cathedral Dome, Palazzo Vecchio and Pitti Palace, is a perfect spot in the evening when the colours of the sunset paint the river.

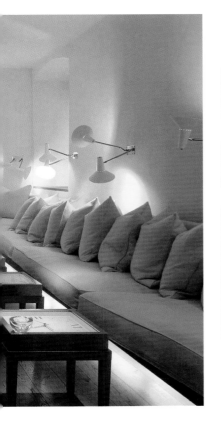

# Gallery Hotel Art
## Florence

*Vicolo dell'Oro 5*
*50123 Florence*
*Tel +39 055 27263*
*Fax +39 055 268557*
*www.lungarnohotels.com*

Just steps away from the Ponte Vecchio, the Gallery Hotel Art is not simply a contemporary boutique hotel, but a modern concept. It is a dynamic gallery showcasing art in the heart of the town that established the first school of fine arts in the world. The hotel is a small island of minimalism in a Renaissance ocean, where modern ideas and art cohabit with international travellers under the discreet signature of the Salvatore Ferragamo fashion group.

Public areas are transformed into multifunctional spaces envisioned to satisfy all the senses. Exhibitions of contemporary art and photography are held in the lobby, library and (The Fusion Bar) Shozan-Gallery. Each room, tastefully assembled using items and materials of superior quality, displays a mixture of style, design and technology to inspire serenity and relaxation.

# Grand Hotel
## Florence

Piazza Ognissanti 1
50123 Florence

Tel +39 055 27161
Fax +39 055 217400

www.starwoodhotels.com

Since becoming a hotel in 1866, the Grand Hotel, a splendid 18th-century former palazzo, has welcomed innumerable celebrities and Florentine aristocracy. Situated on the bank of the river Arno, this magnificent historic landmark bridges the centuries, and offers spectacular views of the river, picturesque churches and palazzos dating from the 15th century. Lavishly restored guestrooms with modern amenities are bejewelled with fresco scenes of Renaissance life, coffered ceilings and crystal chandeliers. Rich fabrics recall the glory of a bygone era. Located on the ground floor, the Restaurant InCanto opens out onto the Piazza Ognissanti, one of Florence's most beautiful squares, and represents an elegant but contemporary style in contrast to the restored Grand Hotel.

# Hotel Helvetia & Bristol
## Florence

*Via dei Pescioni 2*
*50123 Florence*

*Tel +39 055 26651*
*Fax +39 055 288353*
*www.royaldemeure.com*

The passage of time has halted behind the crystal doors of this 110-year-old hotel. Although the Hotel Helvetia & Bristol has recently been elegantly and stylishly modernised, this Belle-Époque hotel has not lost any of its grace. Most rooms have at least one historic work of art on the fabric-covered walls, representing the noblest of Florentine tradition. The public areas are warm with period furniture, 15th-century Italian oil paintings, long curtains and plush velvet sofas. The majestic light of the Winter Garden bar illuminates the history of a unique intellectual club of the 1920s that was frequented by Pirandello, Stravinsky, De Chirico, Montale, Russell and D'Annunzio and his mistress Eleonora Duse.

# Hotel Savoy
## Florence

*Piazza della Repubblica 7*
*50123 Florence*
*Tel +39 055 27351*
*Fax +39 055 2735888*
*www.hotelsavoy.it*

The Hotel Savoy is one of the most sought-after hotels in the heart Florence, the birthplace of the Italian fashion industry. Superbly located, it is within walking distance from the Duomo, the Uffizi Gallery, Ponte Vecchio and the most important fashion houses in the city.

One would expect the old-world atmosphere of a grand hotel by looking at the building's 1893 façade; instead, the interior is warm, stylishly minimalist and modern. Sitting rooms with cream-coloured walls and light, neutral tones throughout are embellished with a funky feel. Valuable contemporary art, most with a shoe theme, is exhibited throughout the common areas and the rooms. Eight sumptuous suites offer the ultimate in luxury, especially the Suite Repubblica that overlooks the historic Piazza della Repubblica.

# The Westin Excelsior
## Florence

*Piazza Ognissanti 3*
*50123 Florence*

*Tel +39 055 27151*
*Fax +39 055 210278*

*www.starwoodhotels.com*
*/westin*

Coloured marble and antique timber, lively frescoes and beautiful terracotta evoke the spirit of Tuscany and the culture of Florence. The magnificent landscape of the surrounding hills, the river Arno and Ponte Vecchio are reflected in the luxurious old-world interiors.

Napoleon's sister Caroline Bonaparte, who was queen of Naples, purchased one of the two palazzos that comprise the hotel in 1833. She renovated it with the help of Giuseppe Martelli, a professor at the Accademia di Belle Arti of Florence. Located on Piazza Ognissanti on the banks of the Arno, The Westin Excelsior combines contemporary accommodation with seven centuries of Florentine history. The classical and sophisticated character of the hotel is balanced by a modern and elegant Art Deco-style bar and restaurant.

# Villa San Michele
## Florence

Via Doccia 4
50014 Fiesole
Tel +39 055 567 8200
Fax +39 055 567 8250
www.villasanmichele.com

Only a few minutes from the centre of Florence, Villa San Michele offers a peaceful oasis among olive groves and vineyards. A villa of impeccable beauty, built on the site of a 15th-century Franciscan monastery, it has been transformed into a charismatic and picturesque hotel. The cream and chocolate façade is attributed to Michelangelo. The monastery's strategic position on the hill of Fiesole, overlooking the Arno Valley, led Napoleon Bonapart to use its library as his headquarters.

Nowadays one can enter through the heavy wooden doors with their massive metal locks and admire the faded portraits of monks from bygone days on the walls and crystal chandeliers in the corridor. The fresco of the Last Supper over the bar was completed by Nicodemo Ferrucci in 1642, and was designed to decorate what was then the refectory of the monastery of San Michele. Whether historic or contemporary, accommodation at Villa San Michele remains fit for an emperor.

# Grand Hotel des Iles Borromées
## Lake Maggiore

*Corso Umberto I 67*
*28838 Stresa*

*Tel +39 0323 938 938*
*Fax +39 0323 324 05*

*www.borromees.it*

Set in an idyllic landscape alongside the peaceful Lake Maggiore and surrounded by the Alps, this grand 1861 palazzo hotel retains the atmosphere of the Belle Époque. Upon entering the Grand Hotel des Iles Borromées, guests are greeted by its sophistication and class. The elegance, style and spirit of its era have been preserved in the refurbishment of the building and its lounges, while the ultimate in modern luxury and comfort has been ensured for the contemporary guest.

Surrounded by lush gardens, ponds and fountains, the Liberty-style façade with its grand marble entrance overlooks the Borromeo Islands. The hotel has hosted many famous guests including artists, actors, politicians, bankers, maharajas, princes and kings. It was a favourite of Ernest Hemingway, who set part of *A Farewell to Arms* here.

# Hotel Ristorante Villa Crespi
## Lake Orta

*Via G. Fava 18*
*28016 Orta San Giulio*
*Tel +39 0322 911902*
*Fax +39 0322 911919*
*www.hotelvillacrespi.it*

In the 19th century a cotton merchant named Cristoforo Benigno Crespi made his fortune by travelling into the heart of Asia. He reached as far as Bagdhad where the exotic city so seduced him with the charms of the orient that when he returned home in 1879, he built a Moorish villa on the spot where he had spent most of his childhood. The palace of his dreams had a minaret and was filled with richly carved horseshoe arches, intricately patterned floors and frescoed turquoise ceilings. A wide park that slopes to the lake surrounds the villa.

In the mid 1980s lawyer Raffaele Esposito transformed the villa into an exclusive hotel, which holds the promise of many unforgettable memories befitting the tales of *One Thousand and Nne Nights*. The hotel boasts a sumptuous restaurant and elegant rooms, all differing in colour and furniture that retain the aura of the kings and queens who frequented the villa in earlier times.

# Villa Aminta
## Lake Maggiore

*Via Sempione Nord 123*
*28838 Stresa*
*Tel +39 0323 933 818*
*Fax +39 0323 933 955*
*www.villa-aminta.it*

The beautiful islands of Isola Bella, Isola Madre and Isola dei Pescatori give the impression of small gems floating in the splendid Borromeo Gulf of Lake Maggiore. In 1832 Admiral Capace Minutolo of the Italian Navy decided to capture this precious view for his beloved wife Aminta, and so created this magnificent private residence.

The Zanetta family, owners of Villa Aminta since 2000, has restored the villa to its original splendour, applying a personal boutique style. Mrs Zanetta directed the elegance and refinement of the decoration and created a charming ambience using chandeliers, Murano glass pieces, stucco works and rich antique furnishings. The lavish surroundings, the beautiful views over the lake and the excellence of the cuisine make up a truly memorable experience.

# Villa d'Este
## Lake Como

*Via Regina 40*
*22012 Cernobbio*
*Tel +39 031 3481*
*Fax +39 031 348844*
*www.villadeste.it*

The most palatial hotel in the world is set in the middle of 10 hectares of heaven, overlooking the blue-green waters of the most romantic lake in the world. The main house, an authentic Neo-Classical villa, was originally built in 1568 as a summer residence for Cardinal Tolomeo Gallio. The trompe l'oeil masterpiece known as the Queen's Pavilion was inaugurated in 1860. In 1873 these two villas were combined to become the Villa d'Este whose luxury and magnificence of a bygone era are maintained even today. Featuring grand staircases, marble columns and silk-covered period furniture, this former residence of European aristocrats has hosted some of the world's most famous poets, painters, musicians, actors and royalty. It is the only place where even the stones flower.

# Excelsior Palace Hotel
## Rapallo

*Via San Michele di Pagana 8*
*16035 Rapallo*
*Tel +39 0185 230 666*
*Fax +39 0185 230 214*
*www.thi.it*

Uniquely located on the Ciappadea Cliff, the Excelsior Palace Hotel enjoys a breathtaking panorama of the Rapallo Bay's blue sea to the east and the headland of Portofino to the west. The historic hotel was the site of the first Italian casino. Even though the casino was relocated to San Remo in 1928, the Excelsior remained the ultimate aristocratic bathing destination. The Duke of Windsor and Mrs Wallace Simpson, King Farouk, King Hussein of Jordan, Rita Hayworth, Ernest Hemingway, D'Annunzio and Eleonora Duse have been among the summer guests that frequent the hotel. The Excelsior has recently been restored to its former early-1900's beauty and elegance. A blend of tradition and refinement, together with spectacular views from every window and terrace, offers quite a memorable experience.

# Hotel Splendido
## Portofino

Salita Baratta 16
16034 Portofino
Tel +39 018 526 7801
Fax +39 018 526 7806
www.hotelsplendido.com

The fabulous unspoiled village of Portofino, with its picturesque harbour full of sailing boats and luxury private yachts, is one of the great summer playgrounds of the rich and famous. Located high above this tiny part of the subtropical Ligurian coast, among exotic gardens of colourful flowers and palm trees, the Hotel Splendido has a commanding presence. This 19th-century villa attached onto the remains of a 16th-century monastery has been a hotel since 1901. The name says it all. Splendido: a grand hotel in every sense, with illustrious guests in a world of elegance and refinement. The Duke of Windsor was the first person to sign the visitors' book and subsequent visits from the most famous and noble families of Europe and the cream of international jetsetters have established its legendary reputation.

# 3 Rooms
## Milan

*Corso Como 10*
*20154 Milan*

*Tel +39 02 626163*
*Fax +39 02 290 00760*

*www.3rooms-*
*10corsocomo.com*

The hotel 3Rooms is an addition to Carla Sozzani's cult fashion complex of stylish shops. It is also a temple to the best of contemporary design, and encompasses a restaurant, bar, café, boutique, bookshop, tea garden and an art gallery. The three pleasant and spacious suites tucked into a corner of the '10 Corso Como' complex are legendary among the fashion community across the globe. American designer Kris Ruhs has set new standards in modern interiors. The individual, white-walled apartments are a showcase of modern design and feature Arne Jacobsen's Swan and Egg chairs, Eero Saarinen chairs, individually designed crystal tables, a Marcel Breurer chaise, an Isamu Noguchi sofa, white carpets with Bridget Riley geometrics, Bang & Olufsen television and music systems, Charles and Ray Eames bedspreads and bathrooms lined with Bisazza mosaics.

# Four Seasons Hotel
## Milan

Via Gesù 6/8
20121 Milan
Tel +39 02 77088
Fax +39 02 7708 5000
www.fourseasons.com/milan

The elegant restoration of a 15th-century former monastery has transformed the Four Seasons into a five-star luxury hotel in the heart of Milan's shopping haven. This precious gem on Via Gesù is just a few steps from La Scala and the couture houses of Via Montenapoleone. Amid the famed Golden Triangle, the Four Seasons Hotel is quite unusual for its atmosphere and design. The original architecture of the monastery has been retained: the courtyard garden is lined by arcades that are now preserved in glass and the lobby with the frescoes was once the monastery's church. Muted colours and subdued, indirect lighting create a warm glow. The historic architectural details blended with contemporary Italian design and American comfort create 118 spacious guest rooms and suites. The hotel's restaurant, La Veranda, frequented by models during the fashion shows, has an elegant and tranquil atmosphere and faces onto the beautiful courtyard.

# Hotel Principe di Savoia
## Milan

Piazza della Repubblica 17
20124 Milan

Tel +39 02 62301
Fax +39 02 659 5838

www.hotelprincipedisavoia
.com

Dominating the Piazza della Repubblica, the Hotel Principe di Savoia, one of Europe's most highly regarded hotels, calls itself the 'Prince of Milan's hotels'. The impressive 1927 Neo-classic landmark near La Scala opera house has been home to international travellers and cosmopolitan society since its opening, yet appears to have remained untouched for the last century. The hotel's grand main entrance is a welcoming gateway to charm and luxury. Marbles in many colours and artistic designs decorate the floors and walls. Crystal chandeliers, statues and the incredible coloured-glass domed ceiling of the convivial Giardino d'Inverno Bar create elegant surroundings. Carefully restored to the highest standards, each of the guest rooms and suites combines the latest innovations in technology and amenities with the elegant 19th-century Lombard style, yet offers the relaxed atmosphere of a private home. The 490-square-metre Presidential Suite, located on the rooftop with its own private pool, sauna, jacuzzi and steam bath, provides pure luxury.

174

**Aleph
Rome**

*Via di San Basilio 15
00187 Rome
Tel +39 06 422901
Fax +39 06 42290000
www.boscolohotels.com*

In the heart of the Eternal City, very close to the famous via Veneto, the stars of the Aleph hotel shine through the walls of what was previously a bank building.

Seven centuries after it was written, Dante's *Divine Comedy* has been reconceived in this unique interior design. Here, heaven and hell allure the guests. Fiery red-coloured sofas in the mysterious black lobby, with its sparkling crystals and shiny metals, represent the burning wells of human souls. On the lobby floor the white, square-shaped Angelo bar appears as a passing cloud, a heavenly drop, the desire of every contemporary demon. The Sin restaurant, where a menu of dishes based on Mediterranean ingredients is served, and the Dioniso wine bar are totally dominated by the red colour of hell. On the floor below, absolute bliss can be found in the luxurious Paradise Spa while on the rooftop, the open-air 7 Heaven restaurant and bar dazzle with spectacular city views.

## Exedra
## Rome

*Piazza della Repubblica 47*
*00185 Rome*
*Tel +39 06 489381*
*Fax +39 06 48938000*
*www.boscolohotels.com*

Exedra, a cosmopolitan haven in the heart of Rome, is a large five-star hotel in one of the most prestigious locations on the Piazza della Repubblica. Built over the ruins of the third-century baths, it avoids the heavy Roman Baroque style of so many other grand hotels of its rating in this city. Classic Italian architecture, with stylish modern elements, soft lighting and fresh flowers combine Neo-classical elegance with modern sophistication. The sunny rooftop garden terrace with the swimming pool overlooks the Fontana delle Naiadi and enjoys spectacular views into Rome's illustrious past including the glorious piazza that houses the ancient Roman ruins of the Diocletian Baths and the Basilica of Santa Maria degli Angeli designed by Michelangelo.

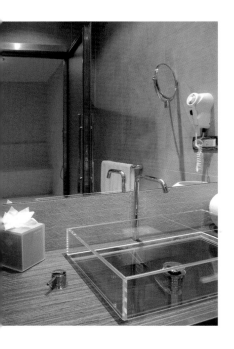

# Hotel de Russie
## Rome

Via del Babuino 9
00187 Rome

Tel +39 06 328881
Fax +39 06 32 888888

www.hotelderussie.it

This chic oasis amid the hustle and bustle of the Eternal City is marvellously located near the Spanish Steps. The simple 1930's-style decor reflects Rome and the Italian character of the hotel, built in 1814.

Hotel de Russie is a new temple of modern style. Its public areas are richly luxurious and contemporary. High ceilings and wide open spaces in neutral tones express the modern version of this grand city hotel. The hotel probably derived its name from Russian dignitaries who sought refuge there, including Igor Stravinsky, the Russian Ballet and the Romanovs. Pablo Picasso and Jean Cocteau were also famous patrons. Hidden from public view, they found a quiet haven in the fragrant blooming Secret Garden, originally designed by the 18th-century architect Valadier. This little tranquil paradise, filled with orange and lemon trees, statues and butterflies, was completed in May 2006 when it became the habitat for the Butterfly Oasis, which is unique throughout the world.

# La Residenza Napoleone III
## Rome

Largo Goldoni 56
00186 Rome

Tel +39 347 7337098
Fax + 39 06 68808083

www.residenzanapoleone
.com

Palazzo Ruspoli, a 16th-century architectural gem on the via Condotti, is one of Rome's best-kept secrets. Located beyond two massive 8-metre wooden doors, an arcade of Doric columns and 100 marble steps, framed by antique busts of Roman Emperors, leads to La Residenza Napoleone III.

Named after Emperor Napoleon III, who lived here in 1830, three magnificent rooms – part of the residence where the famous Ruspoli family lived since 1713 – offer guests all the greatness of a classic Roman palazzo with every modern convenience. Guests are greeted by the owner, Principessa Letizia Ruspoli or her butler, and made to feel at home. Art, antiques, family silver, gold-stencillied walls, reading nooks and cosy couches create the sense of a private museum. The rooms are warm, functional and comfortable, with modern amenities concealed from view. Modern connections for fax and internet are hidden within a walnut desk, while a painting slides away to reveal a plasma television.

# St. Regis Grand Hotel
## Rome

Via Vittorio E. Orlando 3
00185 Rome

Tel +39 06 47091
Fax +39 06 4747307

www.starwoodhotels.com/
stregis

When Ceásar Ritz established Le Grand Hotel in 1894, he created the first technological hotel of its time. Electric lights were installed everywhere, instead of gas lamps, and all rooms were equipped with a private bathroom and heating. Mario Spinetti decorated the ground-floor ballroom, the first ever opened in Rome. At that time the city's population was less than half a million people and the hotel became a temple of luxury for Rome's high society. The hotel changed its name after restorations in 2000, but its charm remains intact. The seductive atmosphere combines Italian- and French-style decoration: lavish interiors with Murano chandeliers, marble busts, hand-painted frescoes, lavish curtains and furniture in Empire, Regency and Louis XV styles.

# Grand Hotel Continental
## Siena

*Banchi di Sopra 85*
*53100 Siena*

*Tel +39 0577 56011*
*Fax +39 0577 5601555*

*www.royaldemeure.com*

In the heart of the ancient medieval city of Siena, just steps away from Piazza del Campo and the pedestrian shopping area, the Grand Palazzo Gori Pannilini, a splendid aristocratic mansion, houses the Grand Hotel Continental. Built by famous Baroque architect Carlo Fontana, this 17th-century palazzo features many glorious frescoes in public areas as well as in several rooms. Arched ceiling frescoes, terracotta floors, prestigious paintings and great period furniture abound. The miraculous grand ballroom on the first floor, decorated with floor-to-ceiling monochrome frescoes, is still as luxurious as it must have been 300 years ago. Entering the magnificent San Cristoforo suite, one is struck by the authentic 15th-century fresco and the rooms with 17th-century walls and vaulted frescoed ceilings.

# Grand Hotel Excelsior Vittoria
## Sorrento

*Piazza Tasso 34*
*80067 Sorrento*

*Tel +39 081 877 7111*
*Fax +39 081 877 1206*

*www.exvitt.it*

Steeped in history, with a cliff-top balcony overlooking Mount Vesuvius and the gulf of Sorrento, the Excelsior Vittoria is truly a grand hotel of the old style, located where the marvellous vacation residence of the emperor Caesar Augustus once stood. A sense of old-world romance pervades the atmosphere: from the Vittoria Dining Room, with its original *fin-de-siècle* decorated ceilings and the Art Nouveau-style Winter Garden, to the Reading Room, with the frescoed ceiling and the Belle-Époque Music Room. Grand Hotel Excelsior Vittoria, owned by the Fiorentino family since 1834 and still operated by its descendents, is located in one corner of Sorrento, lost in time. Surrounded by 2 hectares of semitropical gardens, the hotel combines charming, old-world glamour with a modern flair after a recent restoration. The new Designer Suite is conceived according to contemporary minimal art style. The rest of the rooms are still outfitted with period furniture and elaborate frescoes decorate the ceilings of many suites.

# Palazzo Terranova
## Umbria

*Localita Ronti*
*06010 Perugia*

*Tel + 39 075 857 0083*
*Fax + 39 075 857 0014*

*www.palazzoterranova.com*

Perched high on an Umbrian hilltop, this 18th-century mansion overlooks the misty Tiber Valley. Palazzo Terranova is just a two-and-a-half-hour drive from Rome and one-and-a-half-hours from Florence, ensuring a sense of spaciousness. The hotel is a perfect retreat, offering peace and tranquillity among its 20-hectare park with wild flowers and olive groves. The nine rooms and three suites, which are each named after an opera, are painted in colours that range from light green and fresh violet to soft cream. They have varnished or painted ceiling beams and terracotta floor tiles. Decorated with rich and beautifully crafted furniture, art and paintings, each room is remarkable and unique.

# Bauer Il Palazzo
## Venice

San Marco 1413/d
30124 Venice
Tel +39 041 520 7022
Fax +39 041 520 7557
www.ilpalazzovenezia.com

Bauer Il Palazzo is located in the heart of Venice directly on the Grand Canal. This luxurious boutique hotel is more like a sophisticated home than a hotel. It is an authentic 18th-century palazzo, which cannot simply be considered another addition to the long line of opulent Venetian palazzos offering accommodation to distinguished world travellers.

This hotel is the creation of interior designer Francesca Bortolotto Possati, an astute native Venetian and granddaughter of Armaldo Bennati who purchased the Bauer in the 1930s and has been chairman and CEO of the hotel since 1997. The elegant lobby, decorated in wood panelling and antique Venetian panels, makes a lasting impression that is reflected in the unique decor. Each one of the hotel's individually decorated guest rooms and suites boasts antique furniture, old-style Venetian fabrics and famous Murano glass chandeliers. The Settimo Cielo (Seventh Heaven), a lounge and breakfast terrace located on the seventh floor, offers magical views over Venice and the lagoon.

246

# Hotel Cipriani
## Venice

Giudecca 10
30133 Venice

Tel + 39 041 520 7744
Fax + 39 041 520 3930

www.hotelcipriani.com

Venice has many eponymous luxury hotels but the legendary Hotel Cipriani is the only one that has a swimming pool, a tennis court and a garden setting. The hotel was built in 1956 by Giuseppe Cipriani, who founded Harry's Bar and decided to create a brand new hotel on the island of Giudecca. While not an ancient palazzo, it has a luxurious atmosphere of calm and seclusion, and is only a three-minute trip across the water from the hustle and bustle of the Piazza San Marco. The restored, modern Palazzetto Nani Barbaro that faces the Canale della Giudecca, and the 17th-century-style Palazzo Vendramin, which is linked to the hotel through an historic courtyard and the Casanova Gardens, were added later. The hotel's windows have spectacular views of the Doge's Palace, Piazza San Marco, the Palladian church of San Giorgio and distant islands of the lagoon.

# Hotel Danieli
## Venice

Castello 4196
30122 Venice

Tel +39 041 522 6480
Fax +39 041 520 0208

www.starwoodhotels.com

The coral pink façade of this Venetian Gothic palazzo, a few short steps away from the Piazza San Marco and the Basilica di San Marco, hides a masterfully restored residence that retains its former glory. Of all the hotel lobbies around the world, the Danieli's must be the most extraordinary. It is decorated with medieval frescoes, marble, Murano glass chandeliers, gold and works of art brought from Constantinople by Doge Dandolo after the fourth Crusade. A sweeping marble staircase with Gothic arches climbs up a magnificent towering atrium leading guests to their awe-inspiring rooms. From La Terrazza, the hotel's rooftop terrace restaurant, the panoramas of the Grand Canal and the lagoon are captivating. One can see the Lido and the Adriatic on the horizon, and far beyond one can imagine the Aegean and Byzantium.

# Hotel Gritti Palace
## Venice

Campo Santa Maria
del Giglio
30124 Venice
Tel +39 041 794611
Fax +39 041 5200942
www.starwoodhotels.com
/luxury

The Hotel Gritti Palace preserves stories of illustrious visitors and royal families within its walls. Situated on the Grand Canal, with a breathtaking panorama over the water, this magnificent Venetian palazzo, built for a doge in 1525, offers luxurious comfort. Precious ornaments and a dazzling tableau of chandeliers glimmering against marble enhance the atmosphere. An ornately hand-painted grand piano, intricately woven rugs, marble tiles and finely painted gold-trimmed ceilings fill the lounge area. A portrait of Doge Andrea Gritti distinguishes the space and his aura pervades what was his former residence. Each room, filled with fine authentic Venetian furniture, provides an elegant old-world sense with contemporary amenities and comfort. The terrace of The Club del Doge is a romantic place to dine in the evening, especially when the boat traffic dies down.

# Hotel Monaco & Grand Canal
## Venice

*San Marco 1332*
*30124 Venice*

*Tel +39 041 520 0211*
*Fax +39 041 520 0501*

*www.hotelmonaco.it*

After a long-awaited renovation, this landmark canal-side 17th-century palazzo, acquired by the Benetton group in 1992, was given a new image in 2004. A hybrid of old-world elegance and chic modern design, the Hotel Monaco & Grand Canal offers a warm and friendly atmosphere in elegant surroundings. The reflecting colours of the water and the transparent tones of Venetian glass and mosaic dazzle the guest. The enormous, brightly lit reception area comprises an inner courtyard covered with glass. From the hotel the guests have superb views of the Church of Santa Maria della Salute and the island of San Giorgio. From 1638 to 1774 the building, originally belonging to the Dandolo family, hosted the first 'Ridotto Pubblico' (Assembly Room), a place to which nobility withdrew for gambling, pleasure and intrigue. Giacomo Casanova considered this hotel an ideal setting for his liaisons.

*Index*

# Index

# _I_ndex continued

*Photography and Text by*
*Panagiotis Fotiadis*
*www.fotiadis.com.gr*

Every effort has been made to trace the original source of
copyright material contained in this book. The publishers would be
pleased to hear from copyright holders to rectify any errors or
omissions.

The information and illustrations in this publication have been
prepared and supplied by Panagiotis Fotiadis. While all reasonable
efforts have been made to source the required information and
ensure accuracy, the publishers do not, under any circumstances,
accept any responsibility for errors, omissions and representations
expressed or implied.